BREAKOUT BIOGRAPHIES

IBTIHAJ MUHAMMAD

Muslim American

Champion Fencer

and Olympian

Daniel R. Faust

PowerKiDS press.

New York

Published in 2018 by The Rosen Publishing Group, Inc.
29 East 21st Street, New York, NY 10010

First Edition

Editor: Elizabeth Krajnik
Book Design: Tanya Dellaccio

Photo Credits: Cover, p. 5 Sean M. Haffey/Getty Images Sport/Getty Images; cover, back cover, pp. 1, 3, 4, 6, 8, 10, 12, 14, 16, 18, 20, 22, 24, 26, 28, 30–32 ninanaina/Shutterstock.com; p. 7 (top) Jerritt Clark/Getty Images Entertainment/Getty Images; pp. 7 (bottom), 13 (bottom), 15 (top), 27 (top) Leonard Zhukovsky/Shutterstock.com; p. 9 Ezra Shaw/Getty Images Sport/Getty Images; p. 11 (top) Mintaha Neslihan Eroglu/Anadolu Agency/Getty Images; p. 11 (bottom) D Dipasupil/FilmMagic/ Getty Images; p. 13 (top) KIRILL KUDRYAVTSEV/AFP/Getty Images; p. 15 (bottom) THOMAS LOVELOCK/ OIS/IOC/AFP/Getty Images; p. 17 (top) Mario Tama/Getty Images Sport/Getty Images; p. 17 (bottom) OMAR TORRES/AFP/Getty Images; p. 19 Ed Mulholland/Getty Images Sport/Getty Images; pp. 21 (top), 23, 25 (bottom) Tom Pennington/Getty Images Sport/Getty Images; p. 21 (bottom) hurricanehank/ Shutterstock.com; p. 25 (top) Matt Winkelmeyer/Getty Images Entertainment/Getty Images; p. 27 (bottom) lev radin/Shutterstock.com; p. 29 Noam Galai/WireImage/Getty Images.

Library of Congress Cataloging-in-Publication Data

Names: Faust, Daniel R., author.
Title: Ibtihaj Muhammad : Muslim American Champion Fencer and Olympian /
   Daniel R. Faust.
Description: New York : PowerKids Press, 2018. | Series: Breakout Biographies
   | Includes index.
Identifiers: LCCN 2016057303| ISBN 9781508160588 (pbk. book) | ISBN
   9781508160595 (6 pack) | ISBN 9781508160601 (library bound book)
Subjects: LCSH: Muhammad, Ibtihaj, 1985- | Women fencers–United
   States–Biography–Juvenile literature. | Fencers–United
   States–Biography. | Women Olympic athletes–United
   States–Biography–Juvenile literature. | Muslim women–United
   States–Biography–Juvenile literature.
Classification: LCC GV1144.2.M84 F38 2018 | DDC 796.862092–dc23
LC record available at https://lccn.loc.gov/2016057303

Manufactured in the United States of America

CPSIA Compliance Information: Batch Batch #BS17PK: For Further Information contact Rosen Publishing, New York, New York at 1-800-237-9932

CONTENTS

MEET IBTIHAJ MUHAMMAD

If you watched the 2016 Summer Olympics, you may already know Ibtihaj Muhammad. Muhammad first competed for Team USA at the 2016 Summer Olympics in Rio de Janeiro, Brazil. Muhammad is a Muslim American who made history as the first American athlete to wear a **hijab** during an Olympic competition.

Muhammad has overcome many obstacles in her life, both as a woman and a Muslim American. What was it like for her to grow up as a Muslim in New Jersey after the terrorist attacks on the United States on September 11, 2001, also known as 9/11? How did her family influence and support her decision to become an Olympic athlete? What is fencing and why did Ibtihaj choose to pursue it? The answers to these questions may inspire you to follow your dreams, just like Ibtihaj Muhammad did.

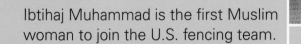
Ibtihaj Muhammad is the first Muslim woman to join the U.S. fencing team.

5

JERSEY STRONG

Ibtihaj Muhammad was born in Maplewood, New Jersey, to Eugene and Denise Muhammad. She has three sisters and one brother, and all five children were expected to participate in athletics. Muhammad's parents believed that playing sports was a way for their five children to confront **discrimination** by giving them a way to be part of their community.

In school, Muhammad participated in softball, tennis, volleyball, and track. The athletic uniforms her teammates wore were an obstacle for Muhammad. As many Muslim women do, Muhammad and her sisters covered their hair and bodies when in public. In order to play on the school teams, the Muhammad sisters wore baggy sweatpants or leggings and long, loose shirts, as well as a hijab.

Ibtihaj Muhammad's parents insisted that their children play sports. Playing sports can be a great way to build **confidence** and learn how to work with others.

Although these outfits followed the rules of the girls' Muslim faith, the sisters were sometimes teased and bullied by their peers. When Ibtihaj (called "Ibti" by her friends and family) was 12, she and her mother passed a local high school. Through the cafeteria windows, they saw students participating in an unfamiliar sport. Muhammad's mother noticed that the students were wearing uniforms that covered their entire body and helmets that covered their hair. Later, they learned that the students were part of the school fencing team.

Muhammad's mother said she wanted her daughter to try fencing when she was old enough. The full-body uniforms would allow Ibtihaj to follow her religion's rules while still taking part in a sport.

Fencing provided Muhammad with a way to participate in a sport and challenge people's perceptions of Muslim women.

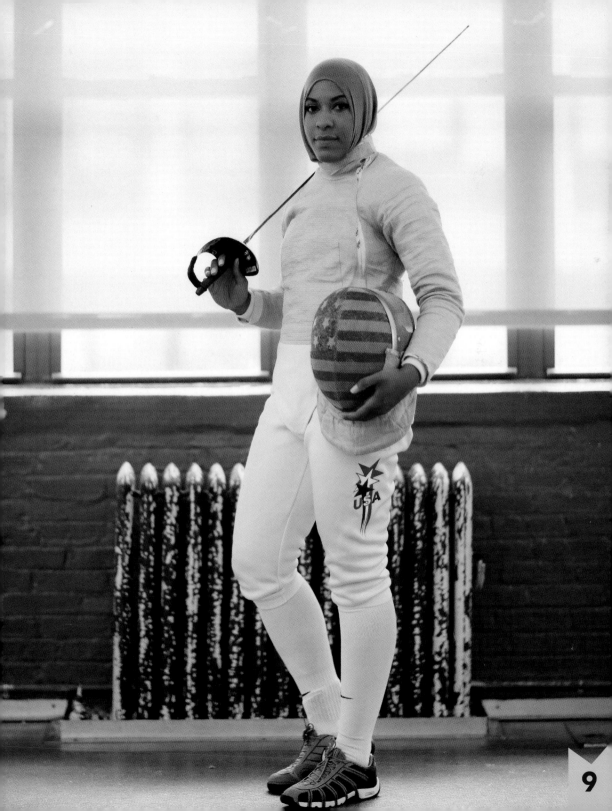

JOINING
THE TEAM

Muhammad started fencing when she was 13. She didn't love the sport at first, but she later changed her mind. In high school, Muhammad was fencing team captain for two years and helped lead her team to two state championships. However, Muhammad found it difficult to win public acceptance, especially when she competed at other schools.

At the time Muhammad started fencing, white athletes dominated the sport. As both a black woman and a Muslim, Muhammad often stood out. She has said it was difficult not having a role model in fencing. Despite the hardships she faced, Muhammad stuck with it. She worked hard and looked for fencing **scholarships** to help her pay for college. In 2003, Muhammad was accepted to Duke University in Durham, North Carolina, on a full scholarship.

ISLAMOPHOBIA

Islamophobia is the fear or dislike of all or most Muslims. This is sometimes based on the belief that Islam is a religion of violence and terrorism. Muslim communities are frequently targets of anger and physical attacks. After the terrorist attacks on 9/11, Muslims living throughout the U.S. were often victims of **prejudice** and violence. Unfortunately, Islamophobia still exists today.

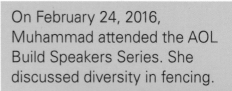

RALLY AGAINST VIOLENCE + EXTREMISM

ONE WORLD, ONE PEOPLE
#United4HumanityLA   AMERICAN MUSLIMS + FRIENDS

On February 24, 2016, Muhammad attended the AOL Build Speakers Series. She discussed diversity in fencing.

EN GARDE!

The modern sport of fencing is based on traditional swordsmanship skills that were practiced across Europe. People used these skills for **dueling**. Fencing originated as a form of military training but became a sport in Italy and Germany during the 14th and 15th centuries. The French later modified the Italian fencing system.

Modern fencing has three forms, based on the style of the weapon used: foil, épée, and sabre. Each weapon has its own rules and **strategies**. In foil events, a fencer may target anywhere on the opponent's **torso**. In an épée event, a fencer can target the entire body. The sabre can be used to target the entire body above the waist, except the weapon hand.

Fencers' uniforms detect when their opponent's weapon has made contact with the target area on their body.

Modern fencers often choose to use one of the three weapons. Ibtihaj Muhammad fenced with the épée before switching to the sabre.

SABRE

THRUSTING AND CUTTING WEAPONS

The foil and épée are thrusting weapons. The fencer jabs the weapon toward the opponent in a forward stabbing motion and the tip of the weapon makes contact with the opponent's body. The sabre is both a thrusting and cutting weapon. The fencer slashes the weapon's edge toward the opponent but can thrust the weapon's tip toward them as well.

OLYMPIC FENCING

Fencing was part of the first modern Olympic Games in Athens, Greece, in 1896. At the time, only foil and sabre events took place. Épée was introduced in the 1900 Summer Olympics in Paris, France. Women's foil events started in 1924. Women's épée events started at the 1996 Summer Olympics in Atlanta, Georgia, and women's sabre events started at the 2004 Summer Olympics in Athens.

In the 1950s, wheelchair fencing was introduced at the Stoke Mandeville Hospital in Aylesbury, England, to help soldiers who had suffered spinal cord injuries during World War II. Wheelchair fencing has been part of the Paralympic Games since they started in 1960 in Rome, Italy. At the 1964 Summer Paralympic Games in Tokyo, Japan, Judith Waterman won silver in the women's individual foil event. She is the only U.S. Paralympic fencing team member to

FENCING TERMS

en garde: "On guard" in French. The position fencers take before a fencing match starts.

feint: A fake attack made to force an opponent to react.

lunge: A common attack in which a fencer moves toward an opponent while pushing off their back leg.

parry: A basic defensive move in which a fencer uses her sword to block an attack.

riposte: An attack made by a fencer after that fencer makes a successful parry.

LUNGE

In wheelchair fencing, athletes' wheelchairs are attached to the floor. Women's wheelchair fencing does not include the sabre event.

FENCING IN COLLEGE

In 2002, Muhammad joined the Peter Westbrook Foundation. This nonprofit organization uses fencing to help develop life skills in young people from poor communities with few resources. Muhammad was invited to train under the Elite Athlete Program in New York City. Muhammad's Olympic coach, 2000 Sydney Olympian Akhi Spencer-El, also studied at the Peter Westbrook Foundation.

Muhammad began studying at Duke University in 2003. In her first year at Duke, Muhammad had a record of 49-8, earning her the first of her three All-American honors. This honor is given to the most outstanding **amateur** players in any given college sport. She also placed second at the Mid-Atlantic/South Regional event. In 2005, Muhammad won several major fencing competitions. She was also named an All-American athlete in 2005 and 2006.

PETER WESTBROOK

An American fencer and Olympic medal winner, Peter Westbrook was born in Saint Louis, Missouri, in 1952. He was a member of the U.S. Olympic Fencing Team from 1976 to 1996. At the 1984 Olympic Games in Los Angeles, California, Westbrook became the first African American to win a fencing medal. In 1996, he was named to the United States Fencing Association Hall of Fame. He started the Peter Westbrook Foundation in 1991 to help **disadvantaged** children through the sport of fencing.

Ibtihaj Muhammad enjoyed success before competing at the 2016 Summer Olympics. Muhammad and her teammates won the women's team sabre event at the 2011 Pan American Games in Guadalajara, Mexico.

EMPOWERING YOUNG ATHLETES

Muhammad graduated from Duke University in 2007 with bachelor's degrees in African and African American studies and international relations. She also studied Arabic.

In 2009, Muhammad began training to **qualify** for the U.S. Olympic Fencing Team. She took the train into New York City every weekday to practice, returning on Saturday mornings to **mentor** a group of about 200 children at the Peter Westbrook Foundation. Whether speaking to a group of children or adults, Muhammad always encourages her listeners to be active members of their community, to dream big, and to think outside the box.

Muhammad's mentoring of at-risk youth is a way to empower kids to take action. She demonstrates that success comes with hard work and dedication.

Muhammad, other members of the U.S. fencing team, and a group of children fenced with First Lady Michelle Obama on Team USA's Road to Rio tour.

TEAM USA

The 2016 U.S. Olympic Fencing Team consisted of 14 athletes: 6 men and 8 women. Even before the Olympic Games in Rio de Janeiro began, many people expected the U.S. Fencing Team to win medals in the team events and the individual events.

Ibtihaj Muhammad made history when she qualified for the team. She would be the first U.S. athlete to compete at the Olympics while wearing a hijab. Muhammad said that one of her goals was to be a role model for **minority** athletes in the sport.

Muhammad's teammates were just as skilled and remarkable. Mariel Zagunis was a three-time Olympic medalist. Dagmara Wozniak started fencing when she was nine years old. Alexander Massialas is the son of a three-time U.S. Olympic fencer.

Despite her individual success, it's important to remember that Ibtihaj Muhammad was a member of a team. The 2016 U.S. Olympic Fencing Team represented the best of the best in the United States.

THE OLYMPIC GAMES

Based on the ancient Greek Olympics, the first modern Olympic Games took place in 1896 in Athens. These Olympic Games featured 280 athletes from 13 countries. They competed in 43 events, including track and field, gymnastics, swimming, wrestling, and fencing. The first Winter Olympics were held in 1924, featuring events such as figure skating, ice hockey, and bobsledding. The Summer Olympic Games and the Winter Olympic Games have alternated every two years since 1994.

THE 2016
SUMMER OLYMPICS

From August 6 to August 14, 2016, fencers from 47 countries came together in Rio de Janeiro, Brazil. These 246 athletes, an equal mix of men and women, competed in the 10 events, 6 individual and 4 team, that made up the fencing portion of the 2016 Summer Olympic Games. The U.S. Olympic Fencing Team won four medals in Rio.

Muhammad competed in two events at the Summer Games—the individual sabre and team sabre competitions. Although she won her first round in the individual sabre event, Muhammad was defeated in the second round by French fencer Cecilia Berder. However, Muhammad and her teammates Dagmara Wozniak, Mariel Zagunis, and Monica Aksamit defeated the Italian team 45-30 to win the bronze medal in the team sabre event.

During the opening ceremonies of every Olympic Games, the athletes from each country march together into the stadium.

MAKING
HISTORY

Before the Summer Olympics began, Muhammad was named one of *Time* magazine's 100 Most Influential People of 2016. U.S. Congressman Keith Ellison wrote, "Ibtihaj embraced what made her stand out, and she's an Olympian because of it."

Muhammad became the first female Muslim American athlete to win an Olympic medal. In addition to the bronze medal her team won in the women's sabre event, the U.S. Olympic Fencing Team also won a bronze medal in the men's team foil event and two silver medals in the men's individual foil and sabre events.

The success of the women's fencing team in Rio brought Muhammad even more media attention. As a representative of the United States and the Muslim American community, Muhammad has devoted herself to being an ambassador for Muslim Americans, African Americans, and women.

SPEAKING OUT

Not all of the press about Muhammad was positive. Muhammad has been the target of racism and discrimination. She has used this new attention to speak out about how Muslims are viewed in countries around the world. By bringing these issues to light, Muhammad hopes to influence people to use more positive language when talking about other cultures and religions.

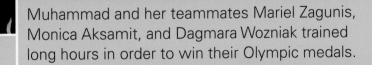

Muhammad and her teammates Mariel Zagunis, Monica Aksamit, and Dagmara Wozniak trained long hours in order to win their Olympic medals.

AN AMERICAN SYMBOL

The 2016 Summer Olympics occurred during the 2016 U.S. presidential campaign. One of the key issues during the campaign was acceptance of the Islamic faith and how the Muslim culture fits into traditionally Western cultures. The continuing threat of the Islamic State of Iraq and Syria, the group commonly known as ISIS, in the Middle East and terrorist attacks blamed on Muslims have contributed to the rise of anti-Muslim feelings in the United States.

As a hijab-wearing Muslim American female athlete, Ibtihaj Muhammad became a symbol of America's diversity and tolerance. This is a role she takes very seriously. Muhammad has spoken about the lack of diversity in fencing and strives to change people's outlook on people

As a woman, a Muslim, and an African American, Ibtihaj Muhammad has become a powerful symbol of the strength of American diversity.

WHAT THE FUTURE HOLDS

The future looks bright for Ibtihaj Muhammad. As a sports ambassador for the U.S. Department of State's Empowering Women and Girls Through Sport Initiative, Muhammad travels around the world to discuss the importance of sports and education.

In 2014, Muhammad decided to try her hand at the fashion industry. She and her siblings started a clothing line called Louella, named after their grandmother, which features clothing that is both fashionable and modest. Muhammad's achievements show that she is not afraid to challenge herself or others.

In a 2016 interview with *Black Enterprise*'s Carolyn M. Brown, Muhammad said, "I want to set the example that anything is possible with **perseverance**." She has truly lived up to this goal and is an inspiration for many

Muhammad believes in the importance of sports education for all children, especially as a way to teach confidence and self-respect in poorer communities.

TIMELINE

December 4, 1985 — Ibtihaj Muhammad is born in Maplewood, New Jersey.

1999 — Muhammad begins fencing at the age of 13.

1999–2003 — Muhammad attends Columbia High School in Maplewood, New Jersey. She helps her high school fencing team win two state championships.

2002 — Muhammad joins the Peter Westbrook Foundation.

2003 — Muhammad starts college at Duke University on a full scholarship.

2004 — Muhammad earns the first of three All-American honors.

2007 — Muhammad graduates from Duke University with degrees in international relations and African and African American studies.

2012 — The Muslim Women's Sport Foundation names her International Sportswoman of the Year.

2014 — Muhammad and her siblings create the Louella clothing line.

April 2016 — *Time* magazine names Muhammad one of the 100 Most Influential People of 2016.

August 2016 — Muhammad competes in the 2016 Summer Olympics in Rio de Janeiro, Brazil. She wins a bronze medal in the women's team sabre event.

GLOSSARY

amateur: Someone who does something without pay.

confidence: A feeling or belief that you can do something well or succeed at something.

disadvantaged: Lacking the things that are considered necessary for an equal position in society, such as money and education.

discrimination: Different—usually unfair—treatment based on factors such as a person's race, age, religion, or gender.

duel: A fight between two people that includes the use of weapons and that usually happens while other people watch.

hijab: The traditional covering for the hair and neck that is worn by Muslim women.

mentor: To teach, give guidance, or give advice to someone, especially a less experienced person.

minority: A group of people who are different from the larger group in a country or other area in some way, such as race or religion.

perseverance: Continued effort to do something despite difficulty or opposition.

prejudice: An unfair feeling of dislike for a person or group because of race, sex, religion, disability, or other differences.

qualify: To show the necessary skill or ability to take part in a sport or contest.

scholarship: Money given to a student to help pay for further education.

strategy: A plan of action to achieve a goal.

torso: The main part of the human body not including the head

INDEX

WEBSITES

Due to the changing nature of Internet links, PowerKids Press has developed an online list of websites related to the subject of this book. This site is updated regularly. Please use this link to access the list: www.powerkidslinks.com/bbios/ibtihaj